Forms

Juliet Dixon

BookLeaf Publishing

India | USA | UK

Presentation by *BookLeaf Publishing*

Web: www.bookleafpub.com

E-mail: info@bookleafpub.com

ISBN: 9789363319233

First edition 2024

ACKNOWLEDGEMENT

Many thanks to my friends, family, and the numerous poets who crafted the guideposts of writing well before me.

Fabric of History - Freeform

hold tight the thread
be pulled through
warp and weft
of time and story

the knobby tweed,
its weave unchanged
yet colored by tales
of slightly varied design

experience noted by buttons
and determined cuffs
while zips of open closed dialogue
escape the cut hem of edit

this sturdy denim holds
quilted comfort of union
rips of discord and
worn patches of laborious task

racks of kin's knit
held in closeted archive,
windows of crafted display,
and lined drawers of memory

Piropos - Tanka 5,7,5,7,7

flowing in whispers
these ribbons of compliments
flirtatiously spilled
run to love-lined reservoir
where I swim in flattery

Scared - Lune 3,5,3

3

sharp inhale
panic's cutting breath
piercing gasp

Flint Hills - Freeform

hazy hills of knee-topped grass
burnt with umber daubs of
furred blotches on flint
lazily floating on verdant swells
rivulets' unnamed routes
of ancient design and cerulean sail

Poetry - Minute 8,4,4,4 8,4,4,4 8,4,4,4 aabb,ccdd,eeff

a metaphor drapes 'round the verse
sometimes perverse
other times grim
delicate hymn

false shroud conceals the translation
imitation
without right wrong
camouflaged song

each stanza holds and hides disguise
a trick applies
the pen's clever
word endeavor

Memory - Alliteration

repetitious rumination
water wheel of faults and phrases
the untender tenacity
of guilt's grip
make savage circles
of unshakable shackles
past's prisoner

Remembering - Villanelle

this song on repeat, whose chorus is sighs
anxiety's breath-letting tune
with recurrent refrain, a past analyzed

this hiss without timbre, no fall and no rise
a slow exhalation, worry strewn
this song on repeat, whose chorus is sighs

ah such concern and oh scandalized
by memories instead of them hewn
with recurrent refrain, a past analyzed

the history's tricky, bad feelings a guise
but to trouble we obsess and croon
this song on repeat, whose chorus is sighs

the hook, the bridge on verses surprise
none as there isn't a boon
with recurrent refrain, a past analyzed

we hem and we haw, the breaths and the cries
yet we can't seem to let go and prune
this song on repeat, whose chorus is sighs
with recurrent refrain, a past analyzed

Traveler - Freeform

grab the bags
packed with history
of rare errors
and unfortunate utterances
the stylish set, memory lined
bulges at faulty clasp
spilling a silken sidewalk
a well-worn path to mistakes' mirror
and hideous reflection
repack, then, with careful separation
folding away the deeds and details
gaps stuffed with
tarnished jewels of recollection
hoist the heavy valise
and walk on

Petrarchan Sonnet

did Petrarch demand this pentameter?
thoughts thought, words formed and extracted,
then caged
wild verse, now captured, fettered, and gauged
by judge and by juries – examiners
the pen, it rests - the verdict: amateur
the gallery gasps, the writer outraged
once powerful words are now disengaged
the cuffs for naught - useless parameter

did he, the bard, whose words blind with luster
have ink of iron, dip quill to provide
the bars of rules and armies of trustors?
this scribe, why stanzas' penultimate guide?
rise rank, seize power, pin badge and muster
order orders where laws and art collide

Humanity - Nonet

Humans incessant repetition
freakishly disagreeable
fascinatingly ugly.
Those who make history,
the pyrite plated
mindsets and deeds
curated
and so
vain.

Unamusing - Limerick

this limerick's not clever nor rude
and humor is not quite the mood
from wit it will stray
and sort of betray
in fact, it is rather subdued

Training - Haiku

take your mark, swimmer
crawl through the turbid current
the pull of duty

Zephyr - Sapphic Verse
11,11,11,5

summers' wind blows pollen through the
Kansan fields
whispering histories of tallgrass pioneers
dreamers through the dusty hopes of wagon
trails
mother of the west

Free - Lune 5,3,5

that ruse called freedom
deceptive
lonely trickery

Actor - Freeform

crack the script
hear the bard's whisper
time's bridge becomes
a catwalk
and most excellent view

bravo, brave thespian
a flawless scene
and individual team
you've split the part
and played them all

and the critic?
a well-practiced role
tinged with as much cruelty
as the playwright's hopeful
benevolence

may your decries be
drowned by ovation
and your reverent bows
be met
with mirrored accolade

Tired - Cinquain 2,4,6,8,2

fatigue
a companion
not exactly a friend
holding tight grasping and clingy
consort

Old - Acrostic

Argue not with the bullies of time and age, for
Creases hold life's magic and
Record numerous tales
Offer instead thanks for the chances
Situations steeped in laughter
That crinkled the surface
Indented the mask
Contouring the character

Model - Shadorma 3,5,3,3,7,5

fakery
the red-lipped smiler
looks out as cruel actor
by artifice and gambit
playing with esteem

The Poet - Oddquain
1,3,5,7,1

draw
penciled strokes
symbolic gesture
the loops and curls of senses
framed

scratch
the eyed scenes
in meanderings
through archives of metaphor's
lines

paint
perception's
pleasing rendition
a figurative tableau
marked

Dodoitsu - 7,7,7,5

daily flip the hourglass
strategize a careful path
this passage paved with eggshells
lined with silences

Polished - Haiku

dry dusty granite
transformed to glistening jewel
by water's caress